DEDICATION

TO GRANDMA,
WHOSE LOVE IS THE SWEETEST INGREDIENT IN EVERY RECIPE,
AND TO ALL THE GRANDMOTHERS WHO MAKE LIFE A LITTLE WARMER,
ONE COOKIE AT A TIME.

ACKNOWLEDGMENTS

THIS BOOK WOULD NOT HAVE BEEN POSSIBLE WITHOUT THE ENDLESS LOVE, WISDOM, AND PATIENCE OF MY GRANDMOTHER, WHO TAUGHT ME THAT FOOD HAS THE POWER TO BRING PEOPLE TOGETHER. THANK YOU TO MY FAMILY FOR SHARING MEMORIES, TASTE-TESTING, AND OFFERING ENDLESS ENCOURAGEMENT. I AM ESPECIALLY GRATEFUL TO MY FRIENDS AND MENTORS WHO INSPIRED AND SUPPORTED ME ON THIS JOURNEY, REMINDING ME OF THE VALUE IN PRESERVING THE STORIES AND RECIPES WE HOLD DEAR.

THANK YOU TO EVERYONE WHO BELIEVES THAT THE KITCHEN IS A PLACE FOR LOVE, LAUGHTER, AND LEARNING. I HOPE THIS BOOK INSPIRES YOU TO SHARE YOUR OWN TRADITIONS AND CREATE NEW MEMORIES WITH THE ONES YOU LOVE.

About the Author

Shatia Godfrey has dedicated her life to the art of baking, blending cherished traditions with professional expertise to create memorable sweet treats. Her love for baking began early, watching and helping her grandmother bake cookies, cakes, and pies—a time filled with warmth and joy that shaped her passion for sharing sweetness with others.

Shatia began her formal journey at Mergenthaler Vocational Senior High School, where she earned a diploma in commercial baking in 2005. This early experience laid a strong foundation, and she further honed her craft at Baltimore International College, graduating in 2007 with an Associate Degree of Applied Science in Professional Baking and Pastry. Eager to expand her knowledge and pursue her dream, Shatia earned an MBA in 2023, combining her love for baking with valuable business skills.

In 2019, she founded Tia Sweet Tooth, a cozy cottage bakery specializing in custom cakes, cupcakes, and sweet treats, each one made with a personal, homemade touch to celebrate her clients' special moments. Through her work, Shatia strives to make each treat a unique part of her clients' lives, capturing memories of joy and celebration in every order.

Cookies at Grandma's House is a heartfelt tribute to the family traditions and recipes that inspired Shatia from an early age. She hopes this book will bring warmth, comfort, and a little sweetness into readers' homes, much like the feeling of enjoying cookies in Grandma's kitchen.

MIA LOVED COOKIES, BUT SHE ALWAYS WONDERED HOW GRANDMA MADE HER'S SO SPECIAL.
ONE DAY, SHE ASKED HER MOM, "CAN WE GO TO GRANDMA'S HOUSE SO I CAN LEARN HOW TO MAKE HER YUMMY COOKIES? PLEASE ?"
AND THAT'S WHERE OUR STORY BEGINS....

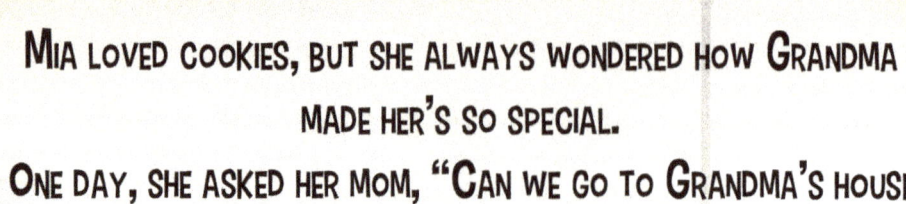

The ride to Grandma's house was always a long ride but, the ride was always filled with excitement and anticipation. Mia knew that arriving to Grandma's house meant hugs, love, and cookies.

Grandma was just as excited to see Mia. With kisses, hugs, and love, Grandma welcomed Mia into her warm home. "Let's start baking your favorite, honey!"

Just like Mia always remember! Grandma's kitchen smell like sugar and butter, and Mia knew it was time to learn what made Grandma's cookies so special.

GRANDMA TOOK OUT HER BAKING EQUIPMENT AND SHOWED MIA HOW TO MEASURE THE FLOUR, CRACKED THE EGGS, AND MIX THE COOKIE DOUGH.

"IT'S NOT JUST ABOUT WHAT GOES INTO THE COOKIE DOUGH," GRANDMA SAID WITH A WARM SMILE. "THE SPECIAL INGREDIENT IS LOVE."

MIA PUT HER ALL INTO WHAT SHE WAS DOING, BUT FELT PROUD THAT SHE LEARNING MORE THAN JUST BAKING. SHE WAS LEARNING THE SECRETS OF GRANDMA'S COOKIES.

After Mia and Grandma put the cookies in the oven to bake, the kitchen began to smell sweet and buttery. Mia could not wait to taste her first homemade cookie with her Grandma's help.

Grandma said, "Now we wait, but I have a little surprise for you while we wait..."

Grandma sat Mia on her lap and told her how she learned to bake the same cookies with her grandmother and how the recipes have been passed down from generation to generation. Mia was happy to know that she was next to have a piece of the family's treasure.

"Now the tradition has been passed down to you, Mia," Grandma said.

Mia beamed, feeling proud and loved.

"I did it!" Mia exclaimed.

I never doubted you for one minute, Grandma said. "From this point on, when you bake, you'll always have a piece of me with you."

DING!

MIA SHOUTS, "ARE THE COOKIES READY!"

GRANDMA NODS AND SAYS, "YES."

GRANDMA LETS MIA TRY HER FIRST HOMEMADE COOKIE. IT WAS WARM, CHEWY, AND SWEET JUST LIKE HOW GRANDMA MAKES IT. "PERFECT, JUST PERFECT," MIA SAYS TO GRANDMA.

As the sun began to set, Mia knew her day with Grandma was coming to an end. This time, she wasn't sad because instead of only getting a cookie or two from Grandma, she left with a box of cookies and Grandma's special recipes to keep forever.

"I'll bake these for you next time," Mia said. Grandma gave her a kiss and whispered, "I'll be waiting, sweetheart."

Mia discovered that baking with Grandma was more than creating her favorite cookies. It was about love, making sweet memories, and continuing the family's tradition.

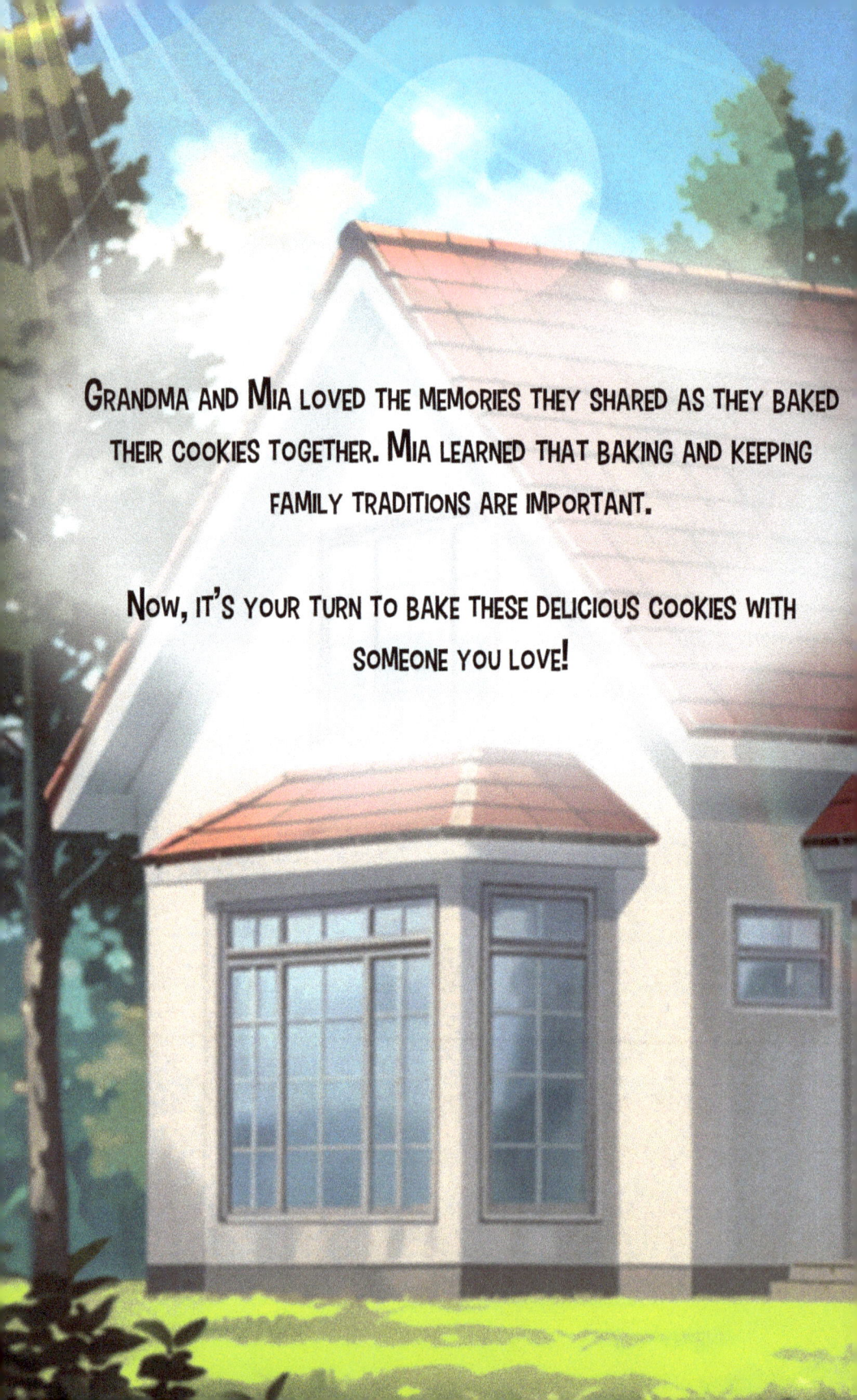

Grandma and Mia loved the memories they shared as they baked their cookies together. Mia learned that baking and keeping family traditions are important.

Now, it's your turn to bake these delicious cookies with someone you love!

Grandma's Classic Sugar Cookies

These buttery sugar cookies are perfect for decorating or enjoying plain with a cup of milk.

Ingredients:
- 2 ¾ cups all-purpose flour
- 1 tsp baking soda
- ½ tsp baking powder
- 1 cup unsalted butter (softened)
- 1 ½ cups sugar
- 1 egg
- 1 tsp vanilla extract
- 3 tbsp milk

Instructions:

1. Preheat the oven to 350°F (175°C). Line a baking sheet with parchment paper.

2. In a medium bowl, whisk together the flour, baking soda, and baking powder.

3. In a large bowl, use a spoon or mixer to cream the butter and sugar until light and fluffy.

4. Add the egg, vanilla extract, and milk to the butter mixture and stir until well combined.

5. Slowly add the dry ingredients to the wet ingredients, mixing until the dough forms.

6. Roll the dough into small balls (about 1 tablespoon each) and place them on the baking sheet.

7. Press each cookie gently with the bottom of a glass or your fingers to flatten slightly.

8. Bake for 8-10 minutes or until the edges are golden brown. Let cool on the baking sheet for a few minutes before moving them to a wire rack to cool completely.

Grandma's Chocolate Chip Cookies

These chewy chocolate chip cookies are a family favorite, with just the right amount of gooey chocolate!

Ingredients:

- 1 ¾ cups all-purpose flour
- ½ tsp baking soda
- ½ tsp salt
- ¾ cup unsalted butter (softened)
- ¾ cup brown sugar
- ¼ cup granulated sugar
- 1 egg
- 1 tsp vanilla extract
- 1 ½ cups chocolate chips

Instructions:

1. Preheat the oven to 350°F (175°C). Line a baking sheet with parchment paper.
2. In a small bowl, whisk together the flour, baking soda, and salt.
3. In a large bowl, cream the butter, brown sugar, and granulated sugar until smooth.
4. Beat in the egg and vanilla extract until well blended.
5. Gradually add the dry ingredients to the wet mixture, stirring until combined.
6. Fold in the chocolate chips with a spoon or spatula.
7. Drop tablespoon-sized dough balls onto the baking sheet, leaving some space between each cookie.
8. Bake for 8-10 minutes or until the edges are golden brown and the centers are soft. Let cool on the sheet for a few minutes, then transfer to a wire rack.

Peanut Butter Cookies

Creamy peanut butter makes these cookies soft, chewy, and so delicious!

Ingredients:

- 1 ¼ cups all-purpose flour
- ½ tsp baking soda
- ¼ tsp salt
- ½ cup unsalted butter (softened)
- ½ cup peanut butter
- ½ cup granulated sugar
- ½ cup brown sugar
- 1 egg
- 1 tsp vanilla extract

Instructions:

1. Preheat the oven to 350°F (175°C). Line a baking sheet with parchment paper.
2. In a small bowl, whisk together the flour, baking soda, and salt.
3. In a large bowl, cream the butter, peanut butter, granulated sugar, and brown sugar until smooth.
4. Beat in the egg and vanilla extract until well mixed.
5. Gradually add the dry ingredients to the wet ingredients, stirring until the dough forms.
6. Roll the dough into small balls (about 1 tablespoon each) and place them on the baking sheet.
7. Press down each ball with a fork, creating a crisscross pattern on top.
8. Bake for 8-10 minutes or until lightly golden around the edges. Let the cookies cool on a wire rack.

Oatmeal Raisin Cookies

Ingredients:

- 1 ½ cups rolled oats
- 1 cup all-purpose flour
- ½ tsp baking soda
- ½ tsp ground cinnamon
- ¼ tsp salt
- ½ cup unsalted butter (softened)
- ½ cup brown sugar
- ¼ cup granulated sugar
- 1 egg
- 1 tsp vanilla extract
- ¾ cup raisins

Instructions:

1. Preheat the oven to 350°F (175°C). Line a baking sheet with parchment paper.

2. In a medium bowl, whisk together the oats, flour, baking soda, cinnamon, and salt.

3. In a large bowl, cream the butter, brown sugar, and granulated sugar until light and fluffy.

4. Add the egg and vanilla extract, mixing well.

5. Gradually add the dry ingredients to the wet mixture, stirring until combined.

6. Fold in the raisins and mix until evenly distributed.

7. Drop spoonful's of dough onto the baking sheet, spacing them out slightly.

8. Bake for 10-12 minutes or until the cookies are golden brown. Let cool on the baking sheet for a few minutes before transferring to a wire rack.